TWO WEEKS TO EMPOWERMENT:

HOW TO TAKE CHARGE OF YOUR LIFE AND FIND YOUR TRUE PURPOSE

KARI FULMEK

ISBN-13: 978-1-9994508-0-9

DEDICATION

I dedicate this book to the love of my life, Sid Chadwick, who stood by me and supported me to believe that dreams could come true.

To my amazing three daughters, Karsyn, Rylee and Raegyn, who inspire me to believe the future is in good hands.

To my late mother, Faye, who steered me on my course to empowerment and never faltered in her life-long support.

CONTENTS

ACKNOWLEDGMENTS

Thank you all for your support in helping bring
this project to completion. I would particularly like to acknowledge:

Content Strategist: Edith Robb
Cover design: Ana Chabrand
Typesetting: Joanna Jablonski with
Ana Chabrand Design House as Project Manager

INTRODUCTION

The most difficult thing about life is how little control you have over the events that flow in and out of it.

I wish I could fix that for you. Sadly, nobody has that kind of power. Maybe it wouldn't be the best gift after all, since life's events are often catalysts for significant positive change.

What I can offer is the power to help you manage your responses to life's ups and downs so they become springboards to your growth and development.

My unusual story and my hard-won skillset gave me insight that allowed me to turn the small equine assisted learning business I started in the isolation of the foothills of Canada's Rocky Mountains into a unique international empowerment company that has clients across the globe.

Equine Connection's Horse Certification Course to train facilitators is the only one of its kind in the world with an attached business component that encourages graduates to empower others through setting up their own businesses. This has resulted in our reach expanding to Australia, New Zealand, England, Denmark, Germany, Dubai and Spain as well as Canada and the United States.

Happy clients have encouraged me to take my story and my methods to a broader audience, and the result is this book.

My goal is that within two weeks, I can empower you to move forward on your journey to achieve the successes in business and in life that you are capable of achieving.

By adapting the stories, advice, and exercises contained in these pages, you can cultivate an attitude that will result in empowered living and the accomplishment of your unique goals.

At the end of each chapter, you will find exercises, most of which you will be asked to do that day. Four of them will take two days to complete, and the result is our 14-day plan to change.

An accompanying workbook is available with 20 additional exercises and space to write in your answers.

This book comes from my heart as well as my brain, skills and training. I genuinely want to inspire you to be empowered and to use your gifts to create the business and the life you have always dreamed about.

Let's move forward together on this exciting journey.

Sincerely,
Kari Fulmek
Master Instructor & Senior Facilitator/Owner
Founder and owner of Equine Connection – The Academy of Equine Assisted Learning Inc.
www.equineconnection.ca

CHAPTER ONE

HAS LIFE KNOCKED YOU OFF BALANCE?

"You are no different than me. We all do amazing work and lead lives that are sometimes very hard and in other ways are spectacular. Sometimes, though, life is so difficult that it knocks you off balance and you feel out of control. Empowerment is the means by which you regain control of your life."
– Kari Fulmek

What is it about our human nature that pushes our happy days together in a hazy blur but allows us to recall our horrible days in vivid detail?

We all carry memories of those moments when our lives were suddenly blackened so dark that we thought we would never see the light again.

The clouds started to gather over me around the end of May, 2011.

At that time I was two years into building up my new business, Equine Connection, the first business of its kind in Alberta to feature the unique Equine Assisted Learning (EAL) Building Block™ program, a horse assisted learning program with a business component.

In 2008 I spent the full year becoming certified in the program and in 2009 enlisted and received amazing support from my mom, Faye, my three daughters, Karsyn, Rylee and Racgyn, and the wonderful man in my life, Sid Chadwick, to put up an arena and secure horses to work with in the program.

Everything I had was invested into building the company to that point. I had a good client base and a $300,000 debt to be paid.

With two failed marriages and two significant career changes behind me, I was ignited to build my business and succeed.

The circumstances leading to my dramatic downfall started around December, 2010.

Mom had been diagnosed at the end of the previous year with a terminal disease which I actually still don't know if she had died from but on the last Sunday in May, it hit me hard that she was getting weaker by the minute.

That same day I had to call the vet because my horse Buddy didn't look right to me. I examined him and I knew there was something seriously wrong. He had mud all over one side of him. The vet said he had likely fallen and to give him some Bute (phenyibulazone, an analgesic to relieve pain). The vet didn't come out to check him at that time.

Fast forward to Wednesday, June 1, and the day the sky fell on me.

I went to get the horses for my equine assisted learning (EAL) program and I saw Buddy lying on the ground. I knew in my heart he was dead. My clients were to arrive in 15 minutes. I rushed to call the vet and they gave me a number for a processor to come and take away Buddy's body. Mercifully my clients cancelled five minutes before they were supposed to show up.

I went to the hospital to cry on my mom's shoulder one last time about the death of my first horse in this business that she supported me so much in but immediately saw that she was not really there any longer. Her body was shaking, and her body was doing horrible things to her. People always say, dying is so peaceful well this was an absolutely horrendous sight. She was fading fast.

Then I hurried back home to meet the processing truck. We had endured days of rain in Alberta and our yard was so muddy that the driver said he could not get his truck to the horse or else he would sink with his truck. He told me I would have to get my tractor and drag Buddy over to where he could get him.

I looked at him in horror. I just couldn't do it. I asked him to wait while I sought help from my closest neighbour. But they were not home so I went to a second one. They were not around either.

I headed back to my place knowing that I could not bear to look at my beloved dead horse lying there all the rest of the day and all night.

I asked the fellow in the processing truck if I drove the tractor could we do it so I just get in my tractor and never have to look back at 'Buddy' and just drive looking at him the whole time, and if he would hook Buddy up to the chain that would drag him to the truck. I just couldn't look. So I towed Buddy to the processor's truck, one of the worst chores of my life.

I made several more trips to the hospital that day and just couldn't emotionally handle seeing my mom the way she was.

At 7 p.m. that night, my aunt called and said that my beautiful mom had died.

Well, it is said that bad things come in threes, but it has been my experience that they come in much bigger and unpredictable bunches.

The darkness reigns

We held my mom's celebration of life Friday, June 3. That same day Arlene, a good friend of my family's, died. By Sunday, June 5, my brother and I started cleaning out my mother's house and the next day, my Uncle Macie died. On Tuesday I went to Arlene's funeral and lost control of myself. It has all been too much for me and I couldn't catch my breath.

But the worst was yet to come.

On Friday, June 10 I discovered that my beloved horse Charlie had a bad nose bleed and I called the vets immediately. I said he wasn't acting like himself at all, and I was worried that he might die like Buddy. They assured me they would come right out.

At the same time, I saw that my horse Poppy was super lame. He had been having trouble for some months and had been seen by vets and had massages and chiropractic care as well as ex-rays, but nothing conclusive showed.

Over the next few days, Charlie still showed no signs of getting better. There was now yellowish, snotty pus coming out of his right nostril all the time.

Through the scoping test the vets discover that Charlie was suffering from a major fungal infection in his guttural sack on the right side. It is a very serious health issue and a rare problem.

The vets say they could perform a $5,000 surgery, but they don't know if it will work. I am already mired in debt for an iffy operation and I just don't have the money. I ask what will happen if I don't get the surgery, and they say he will ultimately die in a pool of blood. I hope against hope they are wrong and Charlie will get a miracle and it just goes away.

During the same visit, Poppy got more tests which included an internal examination, and the vet discovered what was finally wrong with him, it was a broken pelvis. No more riding horse but still believed he had so much purpose left to give in our EAL programs, but his pain was getting excruciating to even move…I had no choice.

Can't take much more

I am frantic. Why is all this happening to me? I believe I am a strong person, but I don't think I can take any more.

I feel helpless in the winds of a cruel fate. I feel that I may not make it, that I am falling flat on my face.

Saturday, July 23 dawns and my Mom's ashes are being buried in Springside, Saskatchewan. I have been asked to do the eulogy and I feel that I will break down when I try to deliver it. I am scared, but I must be strong.

From what others tell me afterwards, I delivered a beautiful tribute to her.

We returned home July 25 and the sun was shining and we had a big family barbecue and my beloved horse Charlie was walking around with nothing coming out of his nose. Perhaps they had been wrong. Perhaps I had been through enough. Perhaps it was all going to be okay. Perhaps my prayers were being answered.

The next morning I am up early. It is only 5 a.m. and I have a steaming hot coffee in my hand when I gaze out into the blackness.

Even before dawn has risen I can see the blood. It is absolutely everywhere.

I call the vets and it takes three needles to bring Charlie to a peaceful end. He is grazing right to his last breath.

I am alternately crying and screaming and numb. I have never felt so out of control of my life.

My horse Pepper died next. I had to have him put down because his leg became so lame and painful and literally dragging his leg to get around and that is no way for a prey animal to live!

In eight short weeks I lost four horses that I loved and that were vital to my business. I had debt up to my eyeballs. In the same time period, I lost my mother, my friend, and my uncle. If I cancelled the courses already booked to take time off to cry and recover, I would have no income.

Is it even possible to rebuild? Had I the courage to do it? Why had life dumped all over me like this?

Then and now

If anyone told me then that I could be empowered to rebuild and my programs would be in demand all over the globe for offering the world's only equine assisted learning course with a special business component and a host of other empowerment programs, I would never have believed them.

If they had told me that through my workshops I would devise programs to empower women who are at a crossroads in their lives and find ways to help youth achieve focus and purpose in their lives, I would never have believed it.

I can't promise you that you can recover from all of your darkest days when you develop your own skills of empowerment, but I know I can help move you onto the right road.

Like my circumstances when events pounded my fledgling business into the ground, you cannot control all the things that life throws into your path.

But you can control yourself, your responses, and your future directions.

It really is all about empowerment, and by that, I don't mean just the accepted definition of a social process through which you will regain control of your own life.

Rather, in this book we will go further and illustrate how over a two-week period of your life, you can challenge your own assumptions about the way things are in your life, and the way they can be.

We will explore where power is and what purpose is, and the importance of growth as a factor of empowerment.

What you will learn

In this book you will learn what your true purpose is in life and how to find the power to live life to that purpose for fulfillment beyond what you can even imagine.

You will learn:
- How to summon the courage to change, the foundation of empowerment
- How to discover your deepest purpose in life
- How to break down the barriers that are holding you back
- How to conquer the self bully that lurks deep within you
- How to open your heart to follow the guides in your life
- How to cultivate an attitude of empowerment
- How to imagine more than your eyes can see
- How to build continual growth into your life
- How to pass on your empowerment to help others

At the end of each chapter, you will be challenged to do one or two actions that will awaken your empowerment and exercise and strengthen it.

I suggest that you pick up a journal or use any one of the many on-line free journal programs like www.penzu.com, www.onlinejournal.com and www.journalate.com to keep track of your journey and exercise responses.

Step one to empowerment:

Please take the time to answer these questions so that you will have a base to return to as you grow your empowerment. One of the essentials of moving forward is having a firm foundation and understanding your current sense of empowerment, however weak or strong it is.

Question 1: How much do you feel in control of your life? You can gauge that by your responses to difficulties. Do they overwhelm you, or do you take them calmly in your stride?

Question 2: Do you recall a specific time in your life when you felt that fate was slapping you down, with each punch worse than the one before? Describe it briefly.

Question 3. What was happening to you and what part of your life was most impacted (family, business, relationships)?

Question 4. Have you experienced a time when you felt there was no way out?

Question 5. Do you believe that you can learn the skillsets to cope with life's ups and down better? Why or why not?

CHAPTER TWO

COURAGE AND CHANGE: YOUR SIGNPOSTS ON THE ROAD TO EMPOWERMENT

"You have to earn your way through life. You've got to do the hard stuff to get to the place that builds your character and allows you to love every second of life, even when it's not going good."
– Kari Fulmek

I started to tell you my story in the last chapter and I encouraged you as a first step to empowerment to start writing yours.

It is important to recognize as a function of empowerment that you have a unique story and every person you meet will have an equally unusual one.

Let's face it. As amazing as life is, it is hard. We all get knocked down not once, not twice but many times after that.

Your story, like mine, will be about moments when you fall down and don't think you can ever get back up again. You get past those low points, but you don't forget them.

You also learn from them about how much strength and power lies untapped within you. You learn how to summon it and channel it and use it to accomplish the impossible.

And when you do that, you have grown so much that you can never fit back into the emotional or mental shape you were before it all started. That is the amazing part of it.

My point-of-no-return is forever marked by the hours after Charlie died when I walked alone out into that huge yard dragging 300 feet of hose and trying to get rid of his blood.

The tears rolled down my face which was already wet from the biting western rain. Water and blood were everywhere, and the earth was not easily accepting and hiding Charlie's lifeblood.

I saw how Charlie had moved all over the yard as he bled. I wept over the path I had led him to death row, the place where the vets put him to his final sleep.

I felt terror when I realized our dogs might have crossed this yard and might they lick the blood that has been drugged by the needles the vet had to give to him to pass onto the next life? Could they die too if they did lick the blood? I called the vets and yes, they sure could! I got them inside until I was able to clean away all the blood that lay on our land.

I started yelling and screaming at God for letting such a thing happen to me. I was ranting and raving, alone in the rain, crazed with grief and fear and helplessness.

I have never seen so much blood and I have never felt so powerless.

When is our burden too much?

Some people think we are only given the burdens we can handle to build our character. I don't buy that. Who can know who will break and who will empower themselves to come back for another round?

Mine isn't a peppy little story of waking up the next morning firmly resolved to rise again and overcome my challenges. Who really does that?

I woke up numb. I woke up still wildly upset, still scared and still lost.

It really took me a year to really get over the trauma of those eight weeks.

That is not to say that I didn't start to take actions towards recovery or that I hated life. Self-pity is no way to live. It's a trap as dangerous as any and a rope that keeps you tied to what you can't change.

But I knew I wasn't healed yet. In fact, in the beginning I became a bit of a hermit. I didn't even want to go to town because people were so kind and they would say "I am sorry for your loss" but I felt so distraught I wanted to yell out "you can't possibly know how I feel."

Everything swirled around in my head. My mother had been my best friend and my business partner. She was only 64 when she died. She was such an amazing woman, so much fun and so kind that she would give a stranger the shirt off her back if it was needed. I had lost her.

My horses were so special to me. I loved them with all my heart and I had lost four of them too.

Slowly I started to rebuild. Word of my story spread, and I was contacted by a lady who offered a four-year-old horse who had never been ridden. I was reluctant to accept; how could she fit into my program? I didn't need a horse with not only a story of being saved twice but being so young, what could this horse offer to me. I needed a reliable older horse with more life skills as I was not a horse trainer. I thought this lady was a little off her rocker for even offering this horse to such an incredible program without more experience. This was definitely not a sign to even consider.

The love of my life, Sid, came home and I said, you have got to come and read this ridiculous letter about this horse.

He said: "Babe, come back and read this letter again as I don't think you have fully understand what this letter is saying. You're looking for a sign of some kind. Did you see what her name is?"

It was Faye, the same name as my mother. It was a sign that I had to find the courage to change.

I started working with the horse and it wasn't an easy fit at first. I had been used to working with an amazing horseman named Eppie Gorger, but a year later as I'm finally starting to really feel once more and surviving 2011, he died suddenly from an accident involving pounding fence posts.

Change is an ignitor of power and learning. I was starting to find the power to move forward but Eppie's death reminded me that I needed to learn more about connecting with my horses if I was going to move along my life journey.

I did not have his depth of knowledge and I knew I had to find that if I was going to progress. I understood that a component of re-igniting my personal power was understanding what I needed to know to move forward.

Finding the courage to accept change

I took Liberty Horse Performance training from an incredible woman, Niki Flundra, and was so impressed with this common sense approach to communicating and connecting at a deeper level with my horses.

I spent almost a year learning as I continued to secure more horses and rebuild my business. With each horse, I built a strong bond to prepare them for future training with my clients.

I began to develop new services and build an amazing team.

Being empowered does not mean that you must do everything yourself when there are others to bring their skills and story to help you go further.

When you are growing and learning and becoming empowered, every day you wake up a little stronger. You expand the potential of what is before you. You create your own path. You consider your story and what would happen if you changed the narrative. You listen to the stories of others and broaden your perspective so you can see a uniqueness to business opportunities.

For me, it was moving more and more into equine assisted business training offered in Equine Connection - Academy of Equine Assisted Learning, Inc.

I knew that nobody else had walked in my shoes and that gave me insight into doing things differently. I didn't just want to train facilitators. I wanted to train people who wanted the same purpose in working with horses to help people and to make a beautiful living as facilitators.

So I started to work with my clients to instruct and teach them not only to learn how to facilitate with horses, but also how to run a business. The first days they spent learning how to facilitate, the last day they learned how to earn a living as a facilitator.

We set up a governing board so our certification could mean something special. We built consistency. We promised our clients we would stay with them as they built up their businesses. We said we would be there with them for life and we delivered on that.
It didn't all go smoothly. We had one person steal from us and that was another setback, but we did what had to be done and moved on.

We added new services, like the Empowerment Series for Women to work with women at risk in Calgary like prostitutes, women just released from jail, and victims of abuse. We had corporate team-building programs to help companies build the gaps from millennials to baby boomers. A youth program to empower young people to be leaders followed and then an Authentic Women's Retreat Weekend to help women find out who they really are and regain their voice and be empowered to move forward. We work with Indigenous youth to help empower them with life skills to move forward with confidence in their lives.

Business grew and my own sense of empowerment returned.

How do you find the courage to get back up and seek empowerment?

I started to incorporate some of my own life lessons into my courses, and in the process, other clients opened up and I also learned from them.

It helped me to understand how empowerment works and how I could pass on that insight to others.

When you start to rebuild after hitting rock bottom, empowerment becomes that inner voice that advises you if you are moving in the right direction or not. Once it guides you to the right path, it reminds you that your path will change and you must find your way each time it does. Change is the constant in our lives.

Perhaps the hardest thing to understand is the idea that as you become empowered, the person you were changes as you grow. It is not like learning to play the harmonica so that you are still you, but now you have an added skill.

Rather, it is a fundamental change within you. You don't go back to being the person that you were before. That person no longer exists, and the new empowered you takes its place.

The thing with empowerment is that you are never done. Once you know how to take charge of your life and live authentically, you keep moving forward. You build a great life, but that involves adding new parts to it and discarding others.

You become a walking, talking empowered evolution of a human being.

Each time you are knocked down, you know you are capable of getting back up so you are less fearful and your recovery time is faster.

Step 2 to Empowerment

Question 1: Where is the path you are currently on taking you? Is that where you want to go? If not, are there options that you could embrace that would move you closer in the direction of the life you want?

Question 2: Have you recently had an experience where you were knocked down to the point that you felt powerless and numb? How did you find the courage to face another day? What thought reassured you?

Question 3: When was the last time that you learned something new? What was it and how has it helped you move further along your path.

Step 3: Your Learning Assessment

In your journal, write down all the formal and informal learning you have accumulated that helps you do your work and live your life.

Do you have learning that you are not using at this point? Is there a way to make it relevant in your life?

When you are looking at where you want to move in the future, what other learning do you need to be more effective once you get there? Is there a way you can start to learn that now, even if you can't see a place to use it right now?

CHAPTER THREE

HOW DO YOU FIND YOUR DEEPEST PURPOSE IN LIFE?

"We all have one purpose and it is simple: we are here to help others."
– Kari Fulmek

The tiny hamlet of Carsland in the province of Alberta where my business is headquartered isn't even marked on most maps.

Situated 20 kilometres east of Calgary, it is a tiny little place nestled in the foothills of the Canadian Rockies.

From my front porch I look out on fields of green, brown, and yellow with generous expanses of wheat, canola and hay. There are cows and horses in various pastures of the welcoming land as it stretches wondrously, sometimes fenced and sometimes free, to curl up at the feet of the rocky base.

Behind it are the mountains that constantly inspire me. With their many peaks and layers, they stretch in unimaginable beauty of greys and purples and blues against a sky that soars to the heavens and beyond.

You can breathe into that endless sky and let your heart soar. There is no rumble of traffic or flashing of neon or drone of endless voices in conflict.

It is the place from which I can think and shape my world as the landscape shapes the universe. It is where I search and find my purpose in life and fulfill my goals.

When you seek to empower yourself and take control of your life, you need to find that spot where the real you emerges and you can immerse yourself in that special place where you use your gifts for your life's productive purpose.

Each of us is born with gifts and as the years pass, our greatest job is to take the opportunities to use them and develop them to the maximum. When we find ways to use our special gifts, we ignite our lives with a passion that keeps us going through the darkest days.

The secret of your purpose

This is your purpose, to identify your gifts, to take them out of you and spread them across the expanse of your world. You must dance to your own music and live life fully and authentically.

Ultimately, the overall purpose for us all, the one we would climb those mountains to understand, is that we are all here to use our gifts to help empower others.

It is not complicated, though millions of people go through their days without understanding it.

Sadly, millions of people also go through life with their gifts still unwrapped inside of themselves. Just as distressing is that millions more allow their gifts to be managed by other people.

Your gift is all you truly have in life, and how you use it is the key to your true empowerment.

Empowerment isn't something you need to seek in the great outside; it is inside of you from the start and is just waiting for you to begin to use your gift to help others.

You cannot be empowered if you do not know what your gift is or how it can be used to the benefit of mankind.

How do you accomplish that?

The power of goals

I believe the road to empowerment starts with identifying our goals and following them. I have been writing down goals since I was a teenager. I imagined what my future would be and wrote it all down.

But I don't go back to them then and check on them. I just let them be. It is clear to me once they are written what they are and I just start stepping forward and amazingly, they happen.

Your goals, once you have formulated them and written them down, become your intention and they guide you from that point forward. You have to imagine what your future could be and make getting to that place your goal.

For example, I always wanted to be an entrepreneur, to work with horses and help other people become empowered. Once I made it my goal, I couldn't even comprehend that it would not happen. Even when I almost lost my business, I knew in my heart I could rebuild it and make it work. It is my gift and my passion and the way I help others in life.

This confidence doesn't mean that I got on the road to where I intended to go right at the start and never took a wrong turn. Quite the opposite is true.

Classrooms were not my space

Where I am now and how I use my gift to be empowered and empower others is a long way from where I started out in life.

I was born in the small community of Yorkton, Saskatchewan April 14, 1966 and was raised my mother, Faye, a hard-working farm girl with a fun-living personality.

My childhood was not filled with trips to Disney World or even fancy holidays, stylish clothes, expensive toys or enrolment in sports and extracurricular activities.

It was rich in its own way, however. I got what some children never receive and that is lots of love and sincere attention.

Faye worked a number of jobs to keep me and my brother Jimmy fed and our bills paid. She taught us her philosophy of life which was: "You can do anything you've ever wanted to do. Just move forward and try it again."

My mother taught me to build my own reservoir of strength within myself and to understand that every person in my life path was special and they should be treated that way.

My mom, my brother and myself moved more than two dozen times when I was growing up and I was forever starting a new school, making new friends, and being picked on and teased. My mom passed on one of her most beautiful gifts to me at that time, and that is to never feel sorry for myself.

Developing coping mechanisms

As a child, I wasn't operating from the place of strength.

Instead of handling the children who picked on me with grace and winning them over, I developed the coping mechanism of being bitchy. It became my wall to protect myself from criticism and judgment.

I felt stupid all the time in school and I just didn't fit in the classroom setting as I got older, even though I stayed with it to get through Grade 12 and graduate.

I learned to lie and use dishonesty to get what I wanted. I did not know what my gift was or how to use it, so I latched onto whatever other tools I could find to survive the harsh atmosphere of one school after another.

I might have gone on that way, despite my mother's love, had I not been exposed to people who had the power to help me unlock my gift and see the impact it has on a life when I could use it to empower others.

Summer camp changed everything

There are many people who show up in our lives and guide us if we are willing to listen. In many cases, your parents are your first and best guides and they empower you to unleash your true gifts on the world.

My mother was amazing and our bond was tight, but she could not do it all or expose me to all of the influences of the world.

A pivotal moment in finding my true self and my gift emerged one holiday when I attended a Christian summer camp. My viewpoint was altered forever when I made the conscious choice to "ask Jesus" into my heart.

In a funny way, it was the day I grew up, because suddenly I understood that I was empowered, that I was accountable for myself and my actions, and I couldn't blame or foist them off on anyone else.

I became fascinated with the idea of karma, that what we put into life comes back to us in many exciting and different ways that I couldn't even comprehend, how. Life is in essence an endless knot of cause and effect and we are all empowered to control its motion.

Our intent and our actions influence our future even while we live in the present. Good intent and good deeds contribute to good karma and happiness in the future. Bad deeds and bad intent leads to bad karma and suffering in the future.

Influential book cemented the direction

Still a teenager, I searched for more signs that I could be empowered and achieve whatever I chose to do in life.

I found them in the book Think and Grow Rich by Napoleon Hill, quite possibly the most amazing book I ever read. It cemented to me the idea that life was going to give back to me what I put into it, and encouraged me to want to put everything I had into it.

During this period I created vision boards of a house I wanted to live in some day, a real home where I could lay down real roots. It took me years, but I live in that house now.

You might say what happened to me over the next few years was all part of my urge to really get started with my life and create my special place on this planet.

Trouble is, I hadn't quite figured it all out yet and the results were not what I had hoped.

The marriage-go-round

Eager to dig into life's possibilities, I decided at the age of 18 to marry the vice-principal of a local school.

That same year when I was working my shift at a local fast food restaurant I found myself staring down the barrel of a gun of the guy who came to rob the place.

The second event had a profound effect on me. It drove home to me just how fragile life is and how quickly it could all end. It is likely the reason I still wake up every single morning and thank-God for giving me this one more day.

The marriage was perhaps less profound. It lasted five years and at 22 when I walked away, I felt like I had just been released from a cage. The freedom was beautiful.

I still didn't know what my true gift was; I still didn't know how to empower myself, but with every experience, I was moving closer to understanding my own power.

I was also getting closer and closer to discovering my gift and what I truly wanted in life.

I bought my first horse.

I desperately wanted to have control over my life and build a business around something I was passionate about. I wanted to work with horses. I had a strong work ethic and my mother's philosophy ringing in my ears. I started to believe I could do anything I wanted to do.

I was moving onto the right path with the horse purchase.

I wanted to get my personal life into growth mode as well so a few short years later I met and married the man who ended up being the father of my three daughters, Karsyn, Rylee, and Raegyn, each born one year after the other for three consecutive years.

It was clear that I was taking a detour when I sold my horse to buy my wedding dress, believing there was no way I could have it all.

I still wanted to be an entrepreneur, however, and I needed money to help support my growing family. At that time I started what would become an 11-year career in sales management with a women's clothing company called Weekenders. It was ideal for me at the time and it taught me incredible skills that would serve me well as I continued to search for my special gift.

Life in the direct sales world

Weekenders at the time was a direct sales company and within it, I built a huge sales team of more than 100 women. It was great for me at that point of my life because I could go to other women's homes and still be a stay-at-home mom because I would put the kids to bed before I went out to work in the evening.

21

In this role, I started to unwrap my personal gift of being able to empower others. I was able to help other women feel great about the outfits they chose for their figures so they could feel motivated, confident and sexy.

A lot of women became empowered to get into the business themselves. They saw how much fun it was and they wanted to own their own businesses too and enjoy a great tax write-off. I built my team quickly and became the first sales manager in the team I was recruited to.

This was a wonderful accomplishment for me. I flew away to conferences every year with the company and they would spoil me rotten like I was the greatest human being on earth. We should all be so lucky with our work!

Lessons to empowerment

Here are two lessons to empowerment that I learned from this point in my life.

First, you can't motivate people. You can only help them so they are motivated to help themselves.

Second, all dreams are absolutely possible within the sales business. You need to know how to sell your products, yourself, and your ideas in life to make your business succeed.

Selling is all about attitude, and when you have a great attitude, you can sell anything to people who need and want your product.

An attitude of empowerment is a huge part of reaching your goals in life.

At this point for me, I had a goal of being a successful businesswoman who travelled with a briefcase on airplanes. That was what I envisioned, and that is what I achieved within this company.

Step Four to Empowerment:

True empowerment is not a lightning bolt that hits you out of the blue and turns on your power. Rather, it is a gradual process of awareness that arises within yourself. It is a thread here and there that you pull, and some threads lead back to the fabric of your life, and others just break and there is nothing left.

In today's exercise, consider aspects of empowerment that can be learned from some of your own life experiences.

For example, what did you learn on your first job that changed your mind about how much power you had?

When did you first get a glimmer that there was a well of power within you if you could only figure out how to draw it out?

Write down some examples of moments that enlightened you about the idea of your own empowerment.

CHAPTER FOUR

BREAK DOWN THE BARRIERS
THAT ARE HOLDING YOU BACK

"Always focus on your intention. Live in the present
and believe that you will achieve your goals."
– Kari Fulmek

For every wave of confidence that arises within you and makes empowerment seem like a possible goal, there is another wave behind it that erodes your confidence and leaves you vulnerable to the whims of others.

So many books have been written about management of others and the leadership of others. Sadly, the most difficult of tasks is the management of ourselves, the leadership of ourselves and the empowerment of ourselves, and that is not as well explored.

You know now that you have a special gift and you are going to be able to use it to help the people around you. You will be empowered to change yourself and others with this gift, but you have to nurture it, and bring it outside of yourself and train it to become all that it can be.

Each life experience gives your insight into how this can be done.

For every step you take in the direction of empowerment, you will encounter the barriers of other people's judgments, opinions and personal desires to hold you back. Sometimes you will even try to hold yourself back!

This chapter is all about breaking down those barriers that try to cover up your gift and keep it from emerging. It is about the blockages that try to hold back your true power and keep you from your real purpose in life of helping others.

Learn to recognize the barriers in your life

For many of us, the harsh criticisms of bullies in elementary school start to build the barriers to holding us back. When we are mocked, our confidence erodes and we start to believe that the bully has all the power and we have none.

We are afraid to stand up to the bully for fear that we will provoke him or her to attack even more violently. We might be only six-years-old, but already we are thinking that if we just stay very small and out of the way and don't antagonize the person trying to control our lives, that we will survive intact.

But we don't. When we grow smaller and turn inside instead of growing more powerful and extending outward, we are not really surviving or even living. We begin to smother our gift, to take the air out of purpose, and to die a little every day.

The hardest aspect of empowerment is to keep others from snatching it from you.

I mentioned earlier that I always felt stupid in school. Even as an adult, I don't fit well in a traditional classroom space, but I know now that I am fully capable of learning and figuring things out and using my gift to teach others.

But many of my teachers failed to enable me to learn. In a way, they created just as many barriers for me as the children on the schoolyard who mocked me.

Once you start to catch a glimmer of insight into what your true power feels like and how genuine empowerment must be, the challenge is to continue to uncover it even if it means making tough choices about getting away from those who put up barriers to your development.

Barriers can be erected even in your home

Some people face barriers within their workplace, some within their social circle, and sadly, some within their own home.

That was how it was with me. As my sense of empowerment and confidence grew with Weekenders, at home in my marriage, the barriers were growing. My life with my husband was volatile; we were like oil and water and the hours were filled with constant fighting instead of mature growth.

I could feel myself growing smaller. I could feel that the power I was gaining was ebbing away when I got home. I understood that I had no choice after five years but to find the strength to exit this marriage.

One night I simply loaded my three babies, aged one, two, and three into the car and left with nothing but the clothes on our backs.

I knew it was going to be tough, but to have stayed would have been tougher. None of us deserves to live in an atmosphere of negativity and unhappiness, always walking on eggshells. Plus I did not want my girls to believe that this is the way a marriage should be and you just put up with it because.

I left and I vowed that night I would never allow myself to be put in that kind of situation again. I was free from ugliness, pain and anger. I was ready to start a new chapter in my life.

Find a way to regain your sense of fun

Fun and laughter are so underrated as essentials of life, but for all of us, they are to our emotional health like food and water to our physical health.

My mother was extraordinary at this point in my life to help me release the feelings of failure I felt over leaving my second marriage and to get my sense of humour and fun back in my family life with my precious babies.

Life is far too short to wallow in self-pity and thinking all those "poor me" thoughts. If you want to live empowered, you can allow yourself a couple of really heart-throbbing cries and then look out on the day you are in, feel the sunshine still warming your face, and get out and live again.

And so it was for me. I started to restore the balance in my life and grow again. I truly did not want another man in my life again. Then I met Sid Chadwick. In fact, I was introduced to him by my mother.

In him I found a person who accepted who I was, who encouraged and enabled me to nurture and grow my gift, and to be the person I could grow to be.

He helped me drop my defenses and accept who I was and feel the power of that person.

I fell truly in love and I am still in love with Sid to this day. He is as nice to me as he was on the first day we met in 1998. We are 18 years apart (he had three older sons when we met) yet we are partners in the same present moment.

He became the father figure to my children and we became a loving, nurturing family again. My daughters were all under the age of four when Sid came into their lives, and they too were able to grow with his steadfast kindness and love.

Growth and change are inevitable

Out of this nurturing environment, we all began to grow again and discover who we were and the lives we were meant to live.

In your life, as in mine, growth and change are inevitable. To deny yourself either of those realities is not to live fully and authentically.

Sometimes you will try to grow or move in a certain direction and it doesn't work. Do not be discouraged by that; it is just a gentle reminder that your direction is in a different place.

Sometimes the impetus to growth is a drastic action or a significant life change, as it was for me leaving my second marriage and forging ahead with three tiny daughters.

Sometimes it is a beautiful coming together of new circumstances and relationships in life that help you find the confidence and strength to move forward, as it was when I became involved with Sid, who is still such an amazing part of my life today.

All of these aspects of my life contributed to a time of fruitful change. It also taught me that while drastic change can be the impetus for growth, finding your balance in life and firming up your foundation is what is needed to really foster growth on a deeper level.

Moving out of your comfort zone

No matter how much you love what you are doing, at some point you must take the time to consider if that is what you should continue doing.

It seems contradictory to even suggest that. But while it is easy to encourage people to leave difficult and challenging places in their lives, it is difficult in the extreme to suggest that happy places also need to be re-examined periodically.

I am not saying you should search for discontent or unhappiness. I merely propose that you need to look at where you are and ensure that it still meets your needs. "Yes, it does" is still a good answer. But if you get a niggling sense that you have settled into something that is less than what you really want in life, then you have to bring that thought out into the sunshine, air it, and look at it from all sides and figure it out.

For me, this was the time when I realized that I was into my 10th year of the Weekenders business and although I had loved it and it had been good for me, it was not the way I wanted to spend the rest of my life. I wanted something so purposeful, so real and that on my last day on earth, I could say, yah, I did good in the world.

My passion for the business was changing, and this happens sometimes. It no longer filled me with purpose as it had once done. I felt a longing for something more grounded, closer to my heart and closer to my home base. And I still wanted to work in the future with horses but I just didn't know what that even looked like.

Sometimes an answer comes when you least expect it. I'm a big believer in taking some days off here and there in life and doing things outside of your normal routine to allow your brain and your thought patterns room to shift and shape themselves in new ways.

A day at the stampede

So it was that I took my three daughters to the Strathmore Heritage Days Stampede for an outing. It is the third largest rodeo in Canada and it was right on my doorstep.

I was excited about the outing. I expected fun fair grounds, lots of great food and a venue for amazing family fun. I was disappointed. Apart from the rodeo events, all it had was an old, run-down snow cone machine and some decrepitated rides.

How could this beautiful community event offer families such a limited experience, I wondered. It was like going to Las Vegas and finding someone had turned out the lights.

My first thought was to complain. I imagined I would write a letter to the local newspaper and say how disappointing the experience had been.

But complaints aren't very useful when it comes to growing, are they? The more I thought about it, the more I considered how I personally might fix it.

This is a good thought pattern for everyone inclined to initiate change. See the problem, override the urge to complain, and instead figure out how it could be fixed. Decide if this is a challenge you want to embrace.

What would I do to fix this, I asked myself? I thought the rodeo part was good, so what if I just focused on creating something on the side like an old-fashioned country fair with a pie-eating contest, dunk tanks, sheep shearing, bales of hay for sitting on, face painting ...even a little tradeshow involving local foods and crafts for people to enjoy?

It would take some financial backing and sponsorships to get things moving, so I decided to see if anyone besides me cared about this. Through my career with Weekenders I knew lots of people in Strathmore, so I visited the companies I knew and asked if they would be willing to help.

I ended up with $20,000 in sponsorship money, three donated ticket booths, and donations for all the other things I wanted to do.

Armed with this amazing support, I went to meet the general manager of the stampede and told him what I wanted to do and the support I had garnered for it.

He sat there surprised and asked this question:

"Are you seriously telling me I can do this and don't have to pay money for it?"
I said "Yep, exactly!"
He said I had a deal as long as I handled the whole set-up.

New career chapter

From anticipation of that day off with my girls to disappointment, from an idea for change to the execution of a solid plan, from a presentation to an agreement, the dance of change began in my life.

I was delighted to succeed in promoting and elevating the once-a-year Strathmore Heritage Days Stampede into a sought-after family event for local residents and those from surrounding regions.

After my first successful year of setting up the country fair idea, I was offered a year-round position with the Agricultural Society as Assistant General Manager.

The third largest rodeo in Canada thrived with the additional attractions. For seven years I remained involved (2004-2010) and managed more than 700 volunteers and 42 committee heads. It did wonders for honing my organizational skills.

I didn't realize it at the time, but it was also channeling my purpose into a new direction.

I started to build a kind of business basis, a menu for executing successful change and what is needed to bring big dreams into reality. I was learned how to be empowered.

People will move with you in life and follow your leadership if you have a clear intention, are consistent in the execution of your intention (as in setting up processes people can clearly relate to), and listen with an open mind to what people are telling you. Everyone has something wonderful to bring to the table. You have an amazing gift, and so do others.

Step Five to Empowerment

Change is tough, but it is essential to living fully and authentically. Falling into the rut of routine without considering if it is still purposeful for you will rob you of your life a day at a time even if it looks pleasant on the surface.

So many of us say that life is a journey, but we live it like we want it to be a destination. If you go through life doing one thing forever, never moving or changing or growing, you might as well say that life is static.

If you change your mindset to decide that change if your friend, that it is the trip to another place that you are looking forward to, then your whole life starts to change.

You have a sense of empowerment that few can enjoy. Change is no longer tough; it is just another few miles ahead on the road of life. You don't have to figure it all out at once. You just have to think one thought, and explore one aspect that doesn't please you anymore. How could you make it better?

In your journal today, trace the eras of your life in personal terms of careers posts, study terms, relationships, etc.

Now look at where you are today. What parts of your life still ignite you? What parts still make you feel that there is a purpose to what you do? What parts don't excite you as you used to? What could you do (instead of complaining) to make them better? Do you have the resources to make the changes you'd like to make in your life?

How could you get those resources? Is there anyone who could help you? For example, if you want to go back to study, are their scholarships available or someone supportive at home to pick up a bit of the slack in day-to-day living?

What would happen if you dipped your toe in the water of change? Are you willing to risk it just to see where it could go?

What would that change be?

CHAPTER FIVE

HOW TO CONQUER YOUR FEAR OF CHANGE

"Ask yourself what's the worst thing that can happen if I make this change in my life? Usually the answer to that is 'it won't work?' Can you survive if it doesn't? Can you survive if you don't even try?"
– Kari Fulmek

The most important thing to know about living is that you only have one life.

Whether you live it fully and try to use your gift to empower others and fill yourself with purpose, or whether you live it timidly with no taste for testing yourself is ultimately your choice.

Either way, we all know that it will end someday, often too soon for our wishes, and our days are done without any chance for a repeat.

It's the reason every morning that I wake up grateful for being given this one more day and conscious that it could be my last.

Some people think that's morbid, but I don't. It is my reminder to live each moment in the present time that it is happening, and not to waste a precious day worrying about things I can't control in the future.

That attitude gives me the courage to listen to my inner voices and try to find purpose in each day. It allows me to dare to use my gift to grow and empower others.

So many people I have encountered are afraid to take the full responsibility for their days. They want to avoid the unpredictability of growth and change without understanding the reality that growth and change will come whether you invite them or not. I always think it would be easier to put out the welcome mat for them rather than have them barge in with an attitude like an invader.

Others believe that they could live a better, more fulfilling life if it wasn't for other people holding them back. It could be the domineering family, the bullying spouse, the demanding children, or even the fear of public opinion.

Two other substantial factors stand between us and true empowerment.

One is fear of financial repercussions; the other is fear of the bully inside us.

Money as the controller

Money is a factor in all our lives. If we don't have any, it is extremely difficult to find the means to sustain ourselves, to keep us sheltered from the weather and nurtured with sufficient food. If we have enough for basic survival standards, everything else is extraneous.

Our inner bully is also present in all of us. It is the voice of our negative self-talk, the promoter of our doubts. It forgets that you have a gift or it suggests that your gift is not adequate or as valuable as the gift of another.

There is only one way to handle these roadblocks to empowerment.

Get your money fears in perspective. Spend some serious time considering money in your life, how much you need for essential survival, how much is owed to others from past decisions, and what your bottom line is.

Be rational about your money, but do not ever let it ever be the sole reason for your life decisions. Money is money; you can always make more. Do not be imprisoned by money as so many people are. We are all rich in life.

I watch so many people tell me their dream and I see the enthusiasm for it in their eyes and it fits with how I see their gift and how it could be used. They tell me this dream when they are 40 and say they are going to save money until they retire at 60 and then pursue that dream.

And I am saddened suddenly, because I know at 60 they must wait until they are 65, and at 65 they have to care for someone who is ill and they will wait just a little longer, and suddenly they don't feel well enough to do it.

There is no age for deciding to pursue your dream, to use the gift you were given and to live purposefully. There is only now.

Who cares that you have a new vehicle (I've never had one!). The things your money buys you have nothing to do with the person you are. Live in the moment.

Don't compare yourself to others. They may have lots of money, but they may still have dreams untapped inside of them. Or maybe they are living their dream and they have money because of that, and they deserve to have it.

For myself, material things became less and less important. I don't have any knickknacks in my house. My bathroom doesn't have a big array of expensive shampoos and toiletries. Success has allowed me to have a lovely home, but it is not full of stuff.

My empowerment does not come linked to my bank account. It comes from being able to step out on the front porch with Sid and sit there and feel the sunshine, breathe in the air and marvel at the mountains. It is our empowerment place.

And I don't let my inner bully fill me with negative self-talk. If I get even a glimmer of that, I shut it down because the more you listen to your doubts and negativity, the stronger they get. You cannot thrive if you live in the darkness of feeling sorry for yourself or mired in regret or a need for hatred or revenge.

You don't need a course to stop yourself from thinking negatively. You just make a conscious choice today to stop it. If it creeps in, as soon as you recognize it, you slam it down and stop it. It will get the message.

You don't have to make all your choices when you are 20

When you graduate from high school or university, everyone asks you what you are going to do with your life, but you really have no idea. You may be one of the lucky kids who has some idea of what your gift is, and you plan a course of studies or work to pursue it.

But for most of us, life is a process of gently uncovering your gift through a variety of challenges and experiments until one day you look at it and it shines and you know confidently what you can do.

34

Some people never get there, and that is sad, but if you work on your own empowerment, you will accomplish it.

For myself, things were starting to change again.

As I moved into my sixth year with the Heritage Days Stampede and the Agricultural Society, the management was asking me to spend more time within the office instead of out in the community.

When my wings are clipped I don't feel happy. When my spirit is smothered a little, I don't feel I can be as purposeful as when I am free.

All of my indicators for living authentically were signaling that it was time for change.

I wanted to feel ignited again, to feel that deep sense of purpose that fills me with energy and fuels my days. I started to think about the kind of work that made me happiest.

I listened to my unease, and to what my heart, my "gift" was saying to me. I wanted to work with horses. I always had, but my own rational thoughts and inner doubts had stopped me.

Horses were my love in life. But I wasn't a horse trainer or specialized in equine discipline, so I didn't know what other option I had for a career with them.

I was looking through a horse magazine and saw an advertisement for an Equine Assisted Learning program where the horses were the teachers. When you took the course, you could help people build life skills as they worked with horses under your guidance.

I decided before my 40s that this was the key to what I really wanted to do with my life: to work with horses and through them, to empower people. I realized once more I am dying and every day is counting and I personally felt there is no more time to waste.

Keep in mind that staying employed was always essential in my life, so I went to the Ag Society and asked for their support as I took this training to become a facilitator with horses in equine assisted learning.

They agreed, and I sealed the deal by giving them one year's notice to find my replacement. I was determined that when I got the training, that would be how I would make my purposeful living.

I've always been an entrepreneur and I knew I could make it work. I didn't know how when I started the training but I knew I could figure it all out as I moved forward with the training.

When doubt hits, ask yourself if the idea is right but the execution is wrong

I began the Equine Assisted Learning course as an on-line learning experience, and it wasn't long before that negative power of doubt started rumbling inside of me. I had experience working with horses that I had acquired throughout the years, but I was just not fully understanding what I was studying.

It sort of made sense in theory, but in reality, I couldn't translate the theory to the practicality of truly understanding how the horse could literally be the teacher.

And as mentioned earlier, when doubt starts, and you listen to it, it magnifies. I was hitting my early 40s and I wanted to position myself in this business. It aligned with my values and my goals, but my doubts started to make me very uncomfortable with this course I set myself on. Did I have it wrong?

Before you let doubt prompt you to abandon what you feel is right, always ask yourself: Is it the idea or the execution of it? Am I on the right course but doing it the wrong way?

So before I made any new decision, I went to Prince Albert, Saskatchewan to see firsthand how this program worked and if it could really be the right business for me. All I would lose if it didn't work was the time, some hard costs and energy I was investing in it.

Preparing for the yearly community event at the Strathmore Heritage Days Stampede was taking some much of my time and my doubt was I don't believe this new business idea with horses is going to work so I called up Tamara who designed and created this incredible program (EAL) and asked her if I could get my money back as I didn't believe this was going to work. She said, 'yes' but she threw in that I would have been the only person in Alberta doing this as a business so now she got my entrepreneurial side.

I ended up making two more trips to Saskatchewan to find peace with my direction and learn more about Equine Assisted Learning (EAL). I couldn't believe the changes I saw in the young people taking the programs. It cemented for me that this way of learning life skills was amazing. The horses truly were the teachers.

I was offered $80,000 to stay with the Heritage Days Stampede and turn it down as I knew in my heart my last breath on earth had to be doing something that I was driven to do with a passion that needed to be fulfilled.

In the end, I knew with everything in me that this was the business that I could be passionate about and succeed in. It would be my purpose to help people in this way and do work that I genuinely cared about.

I spent the entire year of 2009 becoming a certified EAL Facilitator and visualizing the aspects of how my business would work. My deadline for leaving the Ag Society was looming in August of 2010 and I needed to be self-sufficient in business at that point.

My new business, Equine Connection – The Academy of Equine Assisted Learning, Inc. would be the only one of its kind in Alberta with this unique EAL Building Block program to help train facilitators who could leave and then go into business for themselves with understanding in what they do with their certification.

From dreams to reality

There was so much to do to get my business up and operating. A big challenge was to secure the right teachers for my programs…that is, my horses. These 1200 pound instructors had to be seasoned, stable horses who would not over-react to the varied emotions and stimulus coming at them from the youth and adult course participants.

In the beginning, I worked with two of my own horses and rented other horses along with an outside space since I had no facility of my own. During this time four more horses came into my possession and my EAL team was complete.

Money for start-up was needed. Location was my big dilemma. Quotes from neighbouring horse arenas to board and rent the facilities were costly: $2500 to $3000 a month. That was out of the question for a start-up business. Sid, who is a contractor, came up with the idea that we could build a small arena on the three acres where we built our dream home. My daughters were excited and supportive of my dream as was my mother.

Learning to look after myself

Even as I worked to complete my term with the Ag Society and get my new business up and operating, I was reminded that no matter hectic life is, you need to take time to care for yourself.

Most business books never mention that you might need to take a day off during the start-up phase or do something that helps you relax. It seems sinful in our culture to suggest that in the midst of expanding all the energy it takes to think and do what is needed to start a business, that you need moments to yourself.

To live an empowered life so you can empower others, you must simultaneously find or make the time to take care of yourself.

It took me years to understand that it was okay to put myself first and look after my family and business in my life second. If that sounds selfish to you, think about flying on an airplane and being instructed in case of an emergency to secure your own oxygen mask in place before you go to assist a child.

The essential part of empowered living is to understand that it is not selfish to look after yourself first. You help yourself first so that you can help others. You must feed yourself what you need to stay healthy and grounded and know who you are. Then you are in a strong position to be able to help others.

Step Six to Empowerment

You are almost halfway through the process of securing your own empowerment, so it is time to become serious about what components would be needed for your life to be purposeful.

What kind of work makes you genuinely happy? If you had all the free time in the world, what would you do to fill your days? Is there a component of some kind of work in there? How would that work translate to a business offering?

Think about this in great detail. Look at what you love, and look at how it could be turned into a profitable business or career.

Do you need more training before you could go into it full time? How would you acquire that training? Would you be able to continue your current employment as you trained?

What does the market look like for the services or goods you would be offering if you were to open a business? What kind of similar businesses already exist? What could you do that is different or distinctive from them?

Do your research and keep notes about what you discover.

Step Seven to Empowerment

It is time now to make a new life plan. Set your goals for moving towards the purposeful work you want to do and imagine how it will manifest itself. Will it involve establishing a business or securing a different job?

How long from this moment do you think it will be before you can turn your dream into a reality? Throw fear out the window as you do this and believe at this moment that fear doesn't exist.

Will your family or loved ones support it? Why or why not? Can you find a way to work around your unique situation?

If it will involve a business, start now to create a business plan for your new venture.

The Business Development Bank of Canada offers business plan templates to help you if you need assistance. You can access them at: https://www.bdc.ca/en/articles-tools/entrepreneur-toolkit/templates-business-guides/pages/business-plan-template.aspx
     The CBDC offers a fillable PDF business plan option: http://www.cbdc.ca/en/business-plan

You are now a "futurepreneur" and well on your road to empowerment!

CHAPTER SIX

NEED HELP? GUIDES APPEAR IN YOUR LIFE WHEN YOU NEED THEM

"Being empowered means that you can do what you want to do alone. But it also means that you will be guided by others if you let them into your life. With their help, you will do more and you will do it faster. Do not try to live like an island."
– Kari Fulmek

Just when I was feeling empowered that my dream of working with horses would become a reality and I was gathering all my resources to make it happen, Eppie Gorger walked into my life.

He was a true horseman from the Peace River area in Alberta. He wanted to work with the EAL Building Block program and be a part of it. Just as I was seeking my purpose, he was seeking his and his research led him to me.

I had familiarized myself at one point with a concept our Indigenous populations have about asking for guides when we make life transitions, but this was the first time I understood the depth of importance of being open to the guides who enter our lives and taking their help graciously.

Eppie offered me his knowledge and expertise to help me learn more about horses so we could move our program forward globally, not just keep centred in Alberta.

I am forever grateful to Eppie, an amazing calm and quiet man, for his guidance. He helped me immeasurably. He encouraged me to entertain some different ideas about the kinds of horses that should be brought into the herd.

He was supportive, non-judgmental and giving.

Unbelievably, I only had his incredible knowledge and insight for two short years. He died suddenly and tragically due to an accident on his ranch in July, 2012. He was with me as I began rebuilding after my year of tragedy and because of him, I worked hard to step up and be a better horse person. I learned how to create stronger connections with each and every horse I worked with.

Looking back, I see how his influence in my life and his untimely death contributed to pushing me to advance to a different world to connect with horses. What I learned was sacred about how a body works with a horse. I experienced some very interesting situations working all alone with my horses, and each time I gained more insight and so much more confidence.

This time I spent learning and listening to my horses opened the door for me to understand how horses communicate with us to balance us. They actually move energy to each other's bodies, and as I became one with them, they moved energy to mine.

When I was studying and learning in preparation for being better at my business, I felt like I wasn't working. I was just living. It wasn't a killer day to spend hours in company of a horse. I live, breathe and think this business all the time, and these days of working with horses kept me in the moment and helped build my imagination to stretch to all that my business could be.

Earlier I mentioned Niki Flundra of Liberty Training and her amazing influence on me and how she opened my eyes and heightened my skills to work with horses and to connect with them in a completely different way. Once my business had recovered and I had gone global, one of the things I hated most was flying all the way to Australia. I love being there, just not getting there on that long flight that makes me feel like I am in a coffin above water for hours on end. Along came another guide at the right time and right place in the person of Jane Hemingway- Mohr who opened herself to my training and then took it back to expand my work to Australia and New Zealand.

My whole team, which includes Carolyn Charles who has been with me since the inception of my business not only brought a loyalty and trust component that is so important in creating a company but a way to laugh through many challenges and obstacles that continually existed in the first few years of beginning. After my year from hell in 2011 Carolyn's greatest gift was given to me and that was to be able to laugh whole heartily again. My mom and I had so many belly laughs together as we created businesses and I never thought I would ever feel or find this kind of humour in my life once my mom passed on. Carolyn reminds me of my mother is so many uncanny ways and when she helped me to laugh from the belly again I knew what an amazing gift I was given to have her in my life and I am continuously thankful that she is in not only the business but a good friend and indeed family!

My amazing team of facilitators, my clients and my team at the Equine Connection, my equine team and to various degrees my three daughters and Sid, who maintains everything, are guides as well as gifts to helping me achieve my purpose.

Sometimes even students can be guides.

Gaining guidance from others

Sometimes it is difficult for us to understand what our guides are telling us.

In the aftermath of losing my beloved mother and four horses, I sought guidance. What am I supposed to do now, I wondered? What is this life lesson meant to teach me? Should I give up?

The latter went against what I believed in especially since I had worked so hard to get there.

But I desperately needed a sign.

When I arranged to get horses to continue my program after my horse Charlie died, the next day my youthful students arrived with flowers and a hand-drawn card of Charlie. They all gave me hugs and suddenly I knew that despite my despair, I was truly blessed. I went with them to their graduation at the youth centre.

Remember, these are children and youth who had admitted themselves to the program to help get off their addictions to solvents, drugs and alcohol.

These young people stood up and told everyone they were thankful and then they outlined their dreams and their hopes that they would be able to go out into the world and achieve their dreams without addictions. They described how we had all been a family working together and some said they had no other families now that the program was over.

I was absolutely overwhelmed with all of the emotions these young people unleashed and I could not stop crying. I felt love for them and I felt the sign that yes, you are supposed to be doing this work and helping others with your EAL business and you cannot stop now.

I saw clearly that I had a purpose to help as many youth and adults as possible because the program really works. Giving up was never really an option. I have a remarkable program that affects people immediately and empowers them for life. There is no stopping.

My students showed me my way.

Today Equine Connection is known around the world for helping people move forward with their lives. I believe it is because the guidance I receive from others is passed forward with each exercise.

My ultimate guide

The important thing as you move forward and find your personal power in life is to know and appreciate what it is that fuels you to keep going even when the times are tough. What inspires one person and ignites them might not impact another, so you have to find your own way.

In my life, for example, I'm not shy to say that I believe in God and Jesus with all my heart, and the spirituality in my life gives me amazing energy to pass on to others.

Besides thanking God for each day I am given, I also imagine I can see His presence in all of the people that pass through my courses and my life. It reminds me of the Joan Osborne song "What if God was one of us?" (https://www.youtube.com/watch?reload=9&v=7Gx1Pv02w3Q).

In the song we are challenged to consider that if God had a name, what would it be? And would we call Him that to his face? What would he look like in today's world?

It is such a fascinating idea. It is what makes me give a toonie to the fellow who cleans my windshield at the traffic lights at a busy Calgary intersection. Who knows who he really is?

However, still on the spiritual side of things, I absolutely hate the saying that God only gives you what you can handle. I just don't believe that. We are not just submissively being given challenges. We all have free will and we are the ones who chose whether we will live our lives allowing what happens to dominate us, or we rise up and choose our inner power and go on.

Some may fill up their inner reservoir by communicating with nature and feeling the web of life that links us all to the nucleus of the planet.

You need to find what lights your fire and nobody can do that for you. Find the true thing that you believe in that you know will always guide you through the darkest moments, because they appear at some point in all our lives.

Sometimes the spirit and energy of someone you loved who has passed is your ignitor. I can still feel the presence of my mother everywhere I go, for example. I feel her energy.

Even the late Steve Jobs, American entrepreneur and co-founder of Apple, is one of my guides through the wisdom he left in his life. I believe in his premise that a lot of times, people don't know what they want until you show it to them, until you create it for them.

My balance is also maintained by the time I spend with my horses. Their balance gives me balance. Being balanced means knowing what you want to do in this very little life that we have.

In my work, horses are always my guide, gently moving me to the next place, teaching me new things every day. My horses make me ask questions and encourage me to take steps that lead me to a different place.

What happens when you feel empowered

My own empowerment emerged from my life experiences and the influence of all the guides in my life, as yours will.

When you realize that you are in control of yourself, it changes almost everything about your life.

I shoot straight from the hip in life since I have been empowered.

I don't hold stuff inside of me and worry or stress. Worrying doesn't help you be empowered or move forward, because you have no control over worry.

I don't say yes when I want to say no just to avoid hurting someone's feelings. They will not be assisted in their lives by creating a situation where I feel like a martyr in mine.

Being empowered also means accepting there is a beginning and an end to our unique story. The beginning is birth as a living being and for all living beings, the end is ultimately death though many believe our energy may be reborn. Science and research also tells us energy can never die it just continually moves.

With life and death inevitable, what matters and what we have control over is how we move through life.

It is amazing for me to see my life spread from my base at the feet of the mountains and spread now to Australia, New Zealand, Europe, Denmark, and with my travelling schools, to all parts of the United States and Canada. My students come from all over the world as well, from Bosnia and Dubai to southern US and eastern Canada.

Where will your reach spread when you accomplish your personal empowerment?

Step Eight to Empowerment

Who are the guides in your life and what have your learned from them?

Which ones do you consult regularly and how do they help you?

Do you believe their guidance is moving you in the right direction?

Who else could be your guide? How will you learn from them?

Are any of your guides unorthodox, like animals or trees or even those who report to you?

Step Nine to Empowerment

Who or what do you place your ultimate belief in, other than yourself? Who do believe has your back?

Where do you go to fill up your well of power and energy? Is this resource plentiful and accessible?

Write about your reservoir of strength until you are very clear about how it works in your life.

CHAPTER SEVEN

HOW TO CULTIVATE THE
ATTITUDE OF EMPOWERMENT

"You have a story that sets you apart from everyone else. People connect to you because of your story. Nobody has it easy in life. It's how you pull your story together into a cohesive life that defines your empowerment."
– Kari Fulmek

Whether you feel empowered or not in life depends greatly on the inner attitude you have towards yourself and the outer attitude you portray to others.

Your inner attitude sends signals to your brain that you are in charge of yourself and your life, or you are a victim or a person malleable to the wishes of others. It really is as simple as if you feel a sense of power and strength within yourself, you act confidently with power and strength.

Your outer attitude sends signals to others about how they need to respond to you. It emits either a signal of strength, power and decisiveness, or a spirit of uncertainty and vagueness. Others pick up the cues you send and respond to you accordingly.

When I say it is our story that sets us apart, I do not necessarily mean the actual incidents of life that occur for each of us. Sooner or later we all go through hardships, though some are private and some are more visible to others. Our stories set us apart primarily because of how we respond to them.

When you are knocked down in life, that is not your real story. The story that defines your empowerment is what happens in the chapter after you get knocked down. Your audience is intrigued by the story of how you got hit hard in life, and they are inspired by how you handled that and raised yourself not just back to your level, but beyond it.

Explore your third chapter

There is a third chapter to all our stories and so often it is ignored in books and movies about a person's ability to rise again. That third chapter is about how you use what you have learned in the process to help others. When you can reach out and pull others up and help them discover their personal gift, their unique story, and their next chapter, then you have empowered them as well, and that is the true purpose of life.

When I say Equine Connection is different from any other company, it is largely because of our story which you read in the first chapter, how we endured the hardship of losing everything and having to start again. But all that story really tells you is that we didn't have it easy in life, and it is comforting if you did not have it easy either. You know that we were able to pull ourselves back up and not only work in Alberta but all over the world. Our real story, and my real story, is that in the process, we found the way to empower others and that is why every day I feel blessed to live a life of purpose and empowerment.

We must be conscious of this ultimate responsibility to empower others as we empower ourselves at every level of our lives. We cultivate our personal empowerment, our business empowerment, and we must also think of our family empowerment.

I absolutely love being a mother to my three girls, and I feel empowered in that role. The greatest gift I can give them is to empower them to be strong, independent women.

Karsyn, my oldest, went off to university and started living on her own right after high school, I supported her decisions. She decided to quit university; it was just not her passion. She met her now husband and they travelled the world, immersed themselves in different worldly cultures, and gained skills beyond belief that have changed her life. When she had returned from her travels, she had started working with me part time, posting for social media and working with the horses. She eventually got certified, and now is becoming an instructor and working with me in my business. She is a brilliant business person with powerful and unique ways of moving this business forward. My Mom worked with me and now my daughter does, and that fills me with a sense of peace and excitement that the company will live on long after I pass away.

Rylee, my second daughter, left home to study nursing at the University of Lethbridge. She is passionate about helping others and always has been. She too has had no easy road. In her first year representing the school in Volleyball brought a break of her tibia and fibula and the school made her add on one more year of schooling because she was not able to walk and help people in her nursing degree. As she was nearing the end of her degree, she had left her apartment and slipped on the ice, breaking her tibia and fibula and dislocating her ankle on the other leg. She had to get surgery for both of these breaks, bed ridden and on crutches for months. Once again, her nursing degree had to be put on hold, because of this accident. To top it all off, the University was going to yet again, make her complete another year. It took the whole family coming together to fight this injustice and it was no easy task, but in the end she had a plan on how she was going to move forward in her beautiful nursing career and had the perseverance to keep on pushing with finally the support of her University.

Raegyn, my youngest, is studying to be a teacher at the University of Regina, as this has always been her dream career. Now, she is in her final internship in Saskatchewan. When she was in High School, she was bullied by the mean girls in her school and she finally came to the understanding that she would change schools and dedicate herself to her studies for entry into her career with the University. She had saved her virginity for the right one to come along but was out one night with friends, and got into an unwanted situation where she was raped. She called up Rylee and myself immediately, and we took her into the hospital for care. There was a 1 year period of which she could charge her attacker, and she had decided that she was going to do so, as then he could do this to no other girl. He was arrested for a short period of time. The process was long and the cops were not helpful. The cop who was on her case changed out, and from that point on, the process was longer and the cops were less helpful and more blameful. She decided to talk to the judge on her own accord, as being stuck in this horrible past held her from moving forward. The judge understood and respected her decision to drop the case. Now, she's travelling the world and living life without fear, and pursuing her dreams.

I cried as each daughter left. Every year for three years one left right after the other because they were only one year and some apart. I love that they are all still around me and living their lives the way they want to live it. To varying degrees, they are all involved in the business. What more could a mother ask for.

But I knew they had to go away to develop their life skills. If I die tomorrow, they can all survive. They are all empowered because of the consistency with which they were raised.

Cultivating empowerment inside and out

When I worked at Weekenders we used clothes as a means of empowering women. We reasoned that if how we looked on the outside made us feel good, it started an attitude of empowerment. But we wanted also to get inside because that is where true beauty lies. We helped women find their inner beauty and strength so they could move forward with the gifts they were given.

Today my horses are the keys to empowering people of all ages. Each student becomes empowered but it is only when they are willing to learn from the horses.

The horse course, for example, is dedicated to the welfare of the horse and how they communicate with those who are coming to them for help in finding their purpose and their empowerment.

We allow our horses to be the teachers to the programs because they intuitively know the truths. Horses consistently react to the stimulus provided by the participants.

Some of the joys associated with working around horses are that they don't judge, but they constantly assess. Their feedback is honest and instant. Learning to listen, to hear, and to see what horses have to say is imperative to the success of the programs.

We need to understand as we are changing people's lives and we must be an expert in understanding versus guessing. Our equine-assisted facilitators leave with knowledge of how the horse speaks so they can successfully run these objectively driven exercises with results to their communities. Not only do our horses need to feel safe as that is what they are constantly seeking but our human clients too. Without safety, it is most difficult to learn and move forward.

Where the horse fits in with empowerment

How can a horse teach people without the facilitator truly understanding what the horse is saying? Whether you have been with horses your whole life or have just started working with them, you will come away from this certification with a new thought process on how the horse can "speak."

The horse component is essential and a major part of this certification process. It will impact you and how you facilitate your programs. This will be the switch over from using your horses to working with your horses and improving your relationships not only with your horses but all horses. They are the true teachers! They are the bread and butter of our business.

As you become more and more empowered to be in charge of yourself, you need to continue to cultivate the skills of working with others.

For me, I was determined that people would not come and take my course and feel more empowered and then walk away and forget that they could now empower others. That is not the goal or purpose of the work that I do. I want them to carry on and empower other people as they have been empowered.

My intent is to ensure that as each person learns the life skills that empower them; they get an additional component that teaches them how to run their own equine assisted learning program to empower others and make a living.

I invested right from the start in becoming a Certified Master Instructor for the EAL Building Block program which delivers all of these components. From that platform, I had the power to help others who loved working with horses and people and encourage them to have their own EAL businesses. In that way, they could have a positive impact on the lives of others.

Empowerment for me had become a passionate pursuit. I created a format that would give all of my facilitators the tools and information they needed to succeed.

My work life now finds me offering travelling EAL Schools around the world for interested and passionate women (and a smaller number of men) four times a year. In addition, I offer multiple EAL schools from my home base near Calgary.

I am empowered to do the most purposeful job on earth and it drives me every day. I am successful and empowered beyond my wildest dreams, but I will never be rich with money in the bank from my business.

Although we live in comfort, my riches come from seeing other people's lives change every time they encounter one of my results-oriented programs. I am richer for the lives that I have empowered and the change that these people will go out and make in the world.

Step Ten to Empowerment

This is the day that you need to ask yourself the hard questions about what you intend to use your personal power to accomplish.

There is no right or wrong answer to this question. It is against the natural law that we should judge each other.

So if you write down that you want to be empowered to fill up your bank account, that is what works for you and that is the kind of gratification you need, and that is good.

If you write down that you want to be empowered just to fill up yourself so that you can live life fully and authentically, likewise that is a worthy goal and that is good.

If you strive for the highest form of empowerment, which is to empower yourself to empower others, then your life will be rich with purpose and energy and at the end of it all, you can lie on your deathbed and say calmly to yourself, "I did good."

Take the time to establish your intent in this lesson. You are becoming more empowered with each strategy that you choose. What will you do with your new knowledge?

CHAPTER EIGHT

HOW TO IMAGINE MORE THAN YOU CAN SEE IN THIS MOMENT

"If you are living in comfort regularly you are living in the wrong place. Complacency is a horrible place to spend your days. If you are not moving forward, you will stagnate and die a little every day." - Kari Fulmek

In the downtime moments of life, Sid and I live largely on our front porch. Summer or winter, you will find us sitting there staring appreciatively at the land, the mountains and the sky.

One day never looks the same as another, no matter how many times we have gazed on this natural beauty.

Few casual observers are aware that in the grand scheme of the earth's formation, the rocks were actually formed before the mountains themselves roses up. We are looking back more than 1.7 billion years ago.

The actual mountains rose majestically through a period of episodes marked by what geologists refer to as an intense period of plate tectonic activity. That means a lot of motion in the earth, and the last of the episodes was more than 55 million years ago.

The powerful presence of the shale and limestone formations we see that so amaze people from all over the world when they visit Alberta and British Columbia are visible to inspire us because the earth didn't just rest: it moved and changed and evolved.

The mountains inspire me to the core of my being. Rather than seeing them as stagnant pieces of unchanging rock, I understand that they have become something unimaginable over millions of years through their persistent change and evolution.

If rock can move into mountains and change the natural face of the globe, surely we as individuals can grow and cultivate our empowerment and that of others to change the human face of our world.

So much that we can see that is magnificent in this world is the result of the world changing into something our ancestors could never have imagined. And it is like that with ourselves. We can change into newly empowered women and men who have the power to build a world that it better than what we have now, a world we have not yet imagined.

Imagining the impossible

Once you get it into your head and your heart that with your empowerment, a clear intention, firm purpose, and love for what you do, you can also move mountains, there is no stopping you.

As the naturalist and writer Henry David Thoreau put it, "go confidently in the direction of your dreams. Live the life you have imagined."

Being truly empowered means that you can imagine more than what you can currently see around you. Your road is cleared for continual growth, and you do not have to make your life journey on the roads that others have built. You can create your own highway.

We have acknowledged that life is hard and we all get knocked down from time to time. But that doesn't mean it is the end of our story; the knockdowns are the places where we can really start to grow.

Going back to the inspiration of the mountains, I see the challenges in my life as these mountains and it is up to me to figure out how to get around them, or through them, or over them, to reach my destination.

I don't care if anyone else is on the road or where everyone else is going. I know where I am going.

Sometimes you get taken advantage of or have your ideas or methods stolen. Nobody can ever totally protect themselves from getting robbed by the unscrupulous. There's nothing you can do about it and you just have to move forward and keep your own integrity. I'm a great believer in the karma of life that suggests that the person who wronged you will be looked after in some way or another.

I had to put this to the test when I turned 50 and my family and I went to New Orleans to celebrate this milestone. We were at a bar and I bought the first round of drinks to mark the joy of all of us being together. Somehow between the time I paid for them and got back to my table, my wallet was stolen.

In Canadian dollars, it had the equivalent of $1200 Canadian in it. It also had my credit cards, identification, keys and other important items.

My daughter Karsyn was amazing. She got the band to ask if the person who took it could return it. Later that evening, I did get my wallet back, but not the money. Did it spoil our trip? Not at all. Money is money and we were all safe. What I could not replace was the joy of being with those I loved on my milestone birthday so we didn't let the negative thoughts take over our journey. I just hoped that someone needed it more than I and it was being put to good use.

Life is like that. You don't know what each day will bring, and you can't control everything all of the time. Nobody can.

But you can control yourself, your integrity and your passion to keep growing as a person. You can shrug off the cozy blanket of complacency and start to move outside and test the weather there. You can grow.

For example, when I finally got my business going the way it needed to be in Canada and things were going well, I could have just stopped my dream there and drifted into retirement at some stage in the future.

But I know the world is a much bigger place than the foothills of the mountains, and there are many more people who could live fuller lives with self-empowerment, so I began to move to a broader scope. I moved to Denmark, to Germany, to England and to Spain as well as throughout Canada and the United States.

Finding the courage to move

How can you find empowerment in your own world?

You don't have to look far, because you were born with all the tools that you need to use your own gift and power to change your world.

You have a human body to work with, and physical labor is good for the body and soul.

You have a human brain that allows you to envision what does not exist yet and make it real.

You have a heart to feel what you need and what those around you need, and to see how incredible this gift of life is.

You have ears to hear the stories of others and to a voice to tell your own story. You have eyes to see how the stories of others impact them, and a clear intent to act on your own story.

When you are empowered, you cannot get enough of life. You live each day fully and totally, and then you close your eyes and sleep well all night.

In my bedroom there is a picture window so when I wake in the morning, I can see all of life unfolding outside. After thanking God for another day, I am exhilarated that I have another 24 hours to start, and the clear air to breathe and my body to feel all of these things.

I am such a small creature when I stare outside at the mountains, but power is not measured in size.

All my life, I try to see what no one else sees and if you get into that habit, it will empower you many times over.

Develop the values that will aid you

To be empowered means you have the energy to move and effect change in yourself and others, but it does not mean that you will always know what to do with your power.

To be clear about that, you will need to assemble special tools. These are your life values and they will guide you to where your power needs to be directed.

For example, in my life, kindness is huge. I don't believe you have to be unkind to run a global business or to manage all of your relationships. Being kind to yourself and others is the best tool because every time you use it, it adapts to the challenges at hand. Kindness is a remarkable tool.

I need integrity as well. How can I ever build trust and empower other people if they don't trust me? I suggest you use your integrity tool and keep it with you at all times. Do the right thing even when no one is watching and even when they are not expecting it. Go and give to others without expecting something back. When you only do things because you expect them to be returned, you are not living an empowered life, you are merely negotiating.

The perfect win-win is not in negotiating. Rather it is in giving honestly of yourself. You win, and the other person wins. That's how it works.

You also need mental scissors to unhinge your judgment of others and set your opinions free. You cannot judge others because you don't know their stories; you have not walked in their shoes. Some people you meet will be rough around the edges; some will be polished but you sense they are not the person they portray themselves to be.

Greet them with everything you are and learn from them and help them with your kindness. Working with horses and with them I try to help them to be more accepting of who they are and to be more authentic to themselves.

Step Eleven to Empowerment

Today it is essential that you define the tools that you will use to support your empowerment.

These are the values that you take to be true to yourself and that you will apply in deciding where to direct the power or force of your life.

I talked in this chapter about my values that I use as tools. Each person has different values, although some can be the same.

Pick four values that you place the highest value on as tools to support your empowerment.

Consider how you will summon them when you need to make life decisions. Are they of equal importance? Is one a priority and the others all of equal importance? It is important to think clearly about this, because these values and your empowerment will define your intent in life.

CHAPTER NINE

HOW TO BUILD CONTINUAL GROWTH INTO YOUR EMPOWERED LIFE

"My mother's philosophy was to get up and move forward. She told me this over and over again, and I watched how she did it in her own life. She taught me how important continual growth was if I wanted to live an empowered life."
– Kari Fulmek

People who knew me in school likely remember me as bitchy. I developed a tough exterior to protect myself from the criticism and judgment of those around me.

I believed from the beginning that I was unique and I was determined to defend myself and prove my uniqueness by working hard to get what I wanted out of life.

It didn't matter that some of my teachers made me feel stupid. It didn't bother me that some of my classmates were unkind. I knew I would have an amazing life, even though I hadn't worked out all the details.

I grew out of the bitchy defensiveness and the feelings of inferiority. What I didn't grow out of was my ability to accept change easily.

I believe that my attitude towards growth must be a constant in my life came from the guidance of my amazing mother who constantly adapted to growth in her own life and unfailingly supported the concept of growth in mine.

She stressed that we should grow our attitude, grow our skills and grow our understanding of life as a part of growing ourselves.

Continual growth became a part of my life then and it remains a vital aspect of how I see the world and develop my life. I stopped judging myself for not doing it right, right from the beginning as I knew I personally had to go through the entire process to become who I was supposed to be.

Over the years, there were two essential techniques I developed to lay the groundwork for my attitude of fostering continual growth. The first was to envision what my ideal life (including ideal business) would look like and the second was to accept that change is needed in life, whether it is happy or not.

If you know basically what you want out of life and you accept that change will happen and it's okay, you are well on the road to empowerment.

When you cultivate this attitude of continual growth, you become very powerful, because you become an actor in life, not a reactor. You set your own course and refrain from spending all your days trying to catch up from your interaction with the courses others set.

Reframe the unhappy changes

Sometimes the change that appears on your personal horizon is not at all what you were working for. You are struck with illness or your business is impacted by a disaster. Stresses within your personal life distract you from your business goals and your stability wavers.

Sometimes a force for negativity enters your world and begins to colour it with a bad attitude.

When change appears negative, you cannot accept that you are being swept away on the tides of fate and there is nothing you can do about it. No matter how dark and menacing the change is, you must summon your courage and creativity and reframe it.

Take that change and put your positive frame around it. How does it look now? What possible good effects could emerge?

I remember visiting a friend once who had lost many precious family mementoes and items of value in a fire. She stood looking at the ruin and then she smiled and said to me: "for years I have been thinking about minimizing and redecorating. Now I finally have the impetus to do both!"

The art of reframing change is the finest skill you can develop if you truly want to live not only the length of your life, but the width of it. If you want to spread your days as far as they will stretch, and move yourself to the limits of what your special gift will take you, you need to be able to take change on your terms, no matter how unexpected or unwelcome it first appears.

The essence of true empowerment is being able to deal with the fickleness of life and still be true to yourself and your values.

How reframing can work in your everyday choices

I think about how we look at life as I watch so many of the women and men I work with change and grow as they interact with the horses.

Some of them arrive looking and acting powerful on the outside, but if they cannot immediately get the horse to do what they want, they are totally unable to accept this challenge to their power.

Rather than step back and take a new approach if their dictatorial one is not working, they just amp up their forcefulness and are more frustrated than ever when their magnificent teacher just trots away and leaves them to fume.

These are the people who often have a great deal of difficulty taking time out of their office to come to the training in the first place. Moving out of their comfort zone (their desk, their technology, and their willing enablers) is difficult to begin with. When the apparently simple act of leading a horse is not easily accomplished, they become increasingly upset.

It is only when they can reframe their approach, when they can see that the horse does not care that they are the manager, that they have a schedule to keep, that they are powerful somewhere outside of this corral, that the two start to connect and the change becomes positive and the growth powerful.

Reframing your world opens you to growth and empowerment on so many other levels as well.

How many times do you ask people about their life plan and they respond with answers like:
"I have to work for at least five more years."
"I have to do two jobs to pay off my debt."
"I have to stay where I am even though I hate it until my kids are through university."

59

"I have to look after my sick parent (child/spouse) so I have no time to grow myself right now."

What if all of these very real life challenges were reframed and the word "get" was substituted for "have"?

"I get to work for at least five more years. I get to do two jobs to pay off my debt. I get to stay where I am until my kids are through university. I get to look after my sick family member so I get to grow myself at the same time."

Imagine the change in empowerment that comes with altering just one word! What if you altered just one attitude with it, and realized that no matter how hard the change is in your life or how hard the challenge, your solution is not a life sentence for a crime. Rather, it is your thoughtful solution to build a better life. You are empowered to make the changes you need.

So you opt to invest five more years of your life into a certain career so you can firm up your life plan to do something you believe you would prefer in five short years down the road?

So you opt to take a second job to pay down debt and achieve a higher degree of freedom?

So you are willing to sacrifice days doing what you hate for your children? Is that your only option?

So you are choosing to care for a sick family member to practice your love, to magnify your patience, and to grow to the next level of your life?

When you constructively reframe your actions, it forces you to look at them in another way. Sometimes that way turns the negative into the positive; sometimes it just brings clarity that you need to consider other options to the course you are currently taking.

Empowered living is not postponed living

The real secret to living an empowered life is to take charge of every day and live it like it could be your last.
Adopting this attitude has helped me to live mindfully in the present moment, and take the tough decisions for growth that I needed to.

I am not suggesting for a minute that as I grow my business and myself that I have not made some wrong choices or mistakes, but I am saying that I own those choices and so I can live with them.

I chose to leave two marriages. I did not wait until the time was better for a whole list of reasons. I did not excuse myself for staying in a place where I was not able to live fully and authentically for reasons to protect others or because other people might not think I was doing the right thing. I just seized my own power and did what I had to do to live life fully.

I chose to leave two careers and start my own business. I did not wait until the winds of fate convinced me that the economy would be kind to me and that I knew enough to get started without any fear of failure whatsoever. I did not wait until I was a certain age, nor did being at a certain age stop me.

I found the power within myself to do these things and I do not regret them. It allowed me to live my own life, and not dance to the tune of another.

And speaking of dance, only in the last few years have I discovered another passion in my life, and that is to dance. The freedom, the motion, and the control of this art amaze me and it has become another component of who I am. I compete and I train, and I just dance because I love it and it fills me up.

When it occurs to me to try something, I do. I do not sit and wait until I believe I have enough money or time or resources. I jump in and figure it out as I go.

Many self-help gurus advise people to set their goals and put timelines on them and slowly and inexorably work towards them and ultimately, they will accomplish the life they wish to live.

On goals and the compiling of timelines

I look at goals differently. I am in favour of having goals and every so often I sit down and consider where I want to go next with my work and my life and my personal development.

I even write them down because I believe the act of committing them to a list in some way embeds them in my subconscious brain and allows them to guide my thoughts.

But I do not put timelines on them. If I think it is a good goal, I start today. Today is all I have. And every day after, I try to do something that moves me closer to my destination. I cannot change the circumstances and events that brought me to this day, and I have no idea at all if I will have a tomorrow.

So for me, true empowerment means not borrowing against the future, an asset I do not even know I have. It means doing what I believe is right for me today.

It breaks my heart to hear so many people plan what they will do when they retire, and watch them hate every day of work for years leading up to it. How many days are you willing to live in a self-imposed prison for the promise of freedom in some tomorrow that may never come?

I encourage you to practice mindfulness as a component of living an empowered life.

By mindfulness, I mean the ability to be fully present in the moments of your life, to be aware of where you are at all times and what you are doing. You don't have to be overly reactive to life or overwhelmed by it, but you cannot be a person of empowerment if you don't really grasp what is going on in this day of your life.

At some point every day, set aside a little time to practice mindfulness. I often take these moments on my front porch.

In your mindfulness exercise, observe this minute of time just as it is. On the porch, I can feel the sunshine or a chilling breeze on my face, I see the acres of land stretch out to endless heavens and I marvel at my place on this planet. My goal in these moments isn't so much to calm myself or rest, but to pay attention to life.

If stressful thoughts creep in, I do not judge myself for allowing that, but I usher them out again. If I find myself making judgments on others or my own actions, I excuse the thought and gently push it out as well. I return to observe what is around me.

When my mind wanders away again, I calmly bring it back to this moment I am in and give my senses to it to be filled up. I smell the air, feel the breeze, hear the sounds, and see the scope of what is before me.

Many mindfulness practitioners add moments of meditation to their day as well, and if that helps you to stay grounded in the moment, I encourage it. For me, my time with my horses brings me back to the essence of life and authenticity. It is my own form of meditation, I expect.

When you chose to live an empowered life, you need these moments to keep your balance and resolve and avoid sliding back to a mode of living tentatively.

Step Twelve to Empowerment

Practice the art of reframing life's challenges.

Look at the unwelcome change that has come into your life within recent weeks. Take it out as a separate component of your life and reframe it into a different perspective.

How can this change be more positive? How can you reframe it to see it from an entirely different perspective?

Step Thirteen to Empowerment

From this day forward, set aside at least two minutes a day to engage in an exercise of mindfulness.

Find a quiet place free from distractions. Slow your breath by inhaling and exhaling three times. If you have a natural essence that awakens your senses, inhale it at the same time.

Now observe life around you with clarity and without judgment. Try to stay focused only on what you observe.

If other thoughts creep into your reverie, gently guide them out and return to the present. If you start to judge your actions or the actions of others, help them exit as well and return calmly to your connection to the present moment.

You will find the daily practice of mindfulness to be the balance in your growth and continuing empowerment through life.

CHAPTER TEN

PAYING IT FORWARD: PASSING ON YOUR POWER TO HELP OTHERS

"Understand fully what empowerment is. It is not a stick of gold you can shove into the darkness and closed up compartment of a bank vault that will grow with value over time just sitting there. It is only by using it every day yourself and passing it on to others that it gets more and more valuable."
– Kari Fulmek

My work still ignites me 200 percent!

It is beyond humbling to admit that in a world where the majority of people get up and go to a job from which they feel totally disengaged.

Every day I watch human beings interacting with horses to discover that they don't have to live their lives as others tell them to, that they can be empowered to make their own choices and to live life authentically and completely.

With my last breath on earth, this is the job I want to do, to empower others.

It fills me up every single day. I am empowered, and every day I can inspire others to be empowered.

It is the joy of my life to be able to reach out to human beings who feel stuck in their lives and move them forward on their journey. We don't just give them the skills and attitude of empowerment they need to grow; we give them actual life-long help to get into business for themselves as facilitators so they can help others.

We are so pleased to see the growing number of peer-reviewed and published research papers supporting our work because that is giving world-wide credibility to what we have known anecdotally all along.

The thing about being empowered is that as hard as you work to develop it, ultimately it too is a gift. And like all gifts, it grows by being moved forward. When you use your empowerment to help others grow and find their own source of power, there is no work on this planet as purposeful and inspiring.

For myself and my team, working with our horses and through our programs mainly directed at women and youth, there is an opportunity every day to pay forward the gift of empowerment and help others to live fully and authentically. The horses make the magical connection that brings it all together.

So to complete our exploration into empowerment, once you have gained the power over yourself and your own life, how do you continue to grow it and yourself by passing it on to others in more traditional life areas that are not part of the equine assisted learning world?

Empowering others goes beyond being positive in your approach to them and smiling and making encouraging remarks, although all of those things are good starts.

But to really help someone use their special gift and tap into their hidden power, you have to create situations that allow them to challenge themselves. You may want to empower them with all your heart, but only they can uncap their reservoir of strength.

So you have to put them in places where they have to overcome their self-doubt.

It could be as simple as a brainstorming session on how your company is going to progress. It could be a family meeting where everyone is asked for input on how to solve a problem or achieve a goal.

In other areas, you can invite them to events that put them in a situation where they must create. It could be a cooking class or a paint night or a community garden planting or organizing a non-profit event.

Do things as a team and you will be surprised how people begin to come out of their shells. Offer courses and give them opportunities to learn in environments different from their day-to-day life.

Foster participation in life. Invite people to thought-provoking movies or lectures, ask them to go with you to galleries and museums and days of exploration.

Give genuine praise for their accomplishments and respect their ideas.

Remember that empowerment does not mean isolation

Being empowered suggests that you can handle just about anything on your own, but the underbelly of empowerment is understanding that you should not become an island of strength.

If you are really going to use your gift to the utmost and live life fully, you need like-minded people around you.

I couldn't begin to have grown my business to a global force for change if I didn't have an amazing human team with me working with my horses.

Carolyn Charles is a Master Instructor and Facilitator as well as Director of Sales and Marketing. Her special gift is humour, communications and she applies it to recognize and work with many different leadership styles, enabling her to adapt to each client's specific characteristics.

Jane Hemingway-Mohr, is an Instructor and Senior Facilitator and Owner of the Sydney campus - Leading Edge Life Skills. She spent 20 years of her career as a marketing communications manager for a major software firm, handling the Asia Pacific region. These days she is totally committed to the positive effect horses have on people, even those who don't have any affinity for them.

Karsyn Fulmek, my daughter, is an Instructor, Facilitator and Social Media Guru whose love of horses actually brought her to become part of the Calgary Stampede Showriders. She has travelled the world and returned to my delight to join our team not only working with the horses but also keeping our social media trendy and creative.

Brianne Hingley, Facilitator and Development Coach, was only introduced to horses as an adult and became fascinated with their ability to help empower people. She is the driver behind her business of Force Action in

Development as well as coach to other Equine Connection facilitators to help move their businesses forward.

Because of these amazing people, I am able to expand my reach and empower even more people. When I watch their amazing power and creativity at work, it reminds me of how limited I would be if I believed I had to do everything myself.

I don't think it is a coincidence that so many of my team members are professional communicators as well as amazing facilitators. We know that communication is vital to our empowerment. We all need to voice our opinions and ideas. In companies where that is not encouraged, it would be very difficult to have real growth.

Practicing empowerment in your life

In this book, my goal is to share with you my story of empowerment for myself and others, and in the process, to illustrate to you how you can find your own gift and be empowered to use it in your own life.

We all have our stories to tell, but in the end there is just one story and that is to find the means and the skill to life our lives purposefully and with authenticity.

We must guard against letting a quality as vital as empowerment become a buzzword in a never-ending conversation about trendy social values.

Empowerment is as vital now as it has ever been, and without hesitation, I can say it will be vital to the next generation and the one that follows and on into infinity.

What we need to remember through each decade is that empowerment is not an immovable, static thing that once earned, is forever with us. We have to constantly protect it, practice it and persist in developing it still further if we are to guard its value to us and how we live our lives.

It is not a force you use to hold your own against others; it is a tool you turn on yourself and use it to challenge your thinking, your assumptions, and your mode of living. It is not something you pull out for business meetings or career planning and leave on the doorstep of your home life. It is multi-dimensional and needs to be used in every aspect of how you live and breathe on this planet.

Yes, you have gained power over your life and your work, but you must be conscious that that power must keep changing and evolving if it is to continue to be useful to you.

Power in the sense of empowerment is not about control and domination in the strictest sense. An empowered life is not one lived at the expense of another, as in a power situation in the traditional workplace where the boss is the source of power and the workers must do what the boss says. It isn't like that at all.

Living as an empowered individual merely means that you have power over your own life, that you can use power in your community and in a broader society overall by doing the things that you believe matter to you and in this world.

Be conscious of the need for change

There are complex problems in today's world that need solving, and no one of us can purport to have all the answers, though we may have insight and skills to put out there to help find the solution.

By ensuring that we are empowered to feel comfortable contributing, to feel ignited to do our work, and by empowering others, we can become a force to change the world and find the answers to those big questions that daunt our development as a civilization.

Being empowered means being able to work towards solutions with respect for the opinions and skills of others, and to be open to listening without judgment to the contributions of others as we insist they hear us out.

The empowered part of me acknowledges that there is a need for change as my own company grows. We are discussing new facilities and new countries to expand into. We are honing our programs and discussing whether there are other things we can do to meet the needs we see around us.

How can you translate your feeling of empowerment into your workplace, into your family, into your community and into the broader world?
How can you use your special gifts to empower others?

To do that, you must first engage with others, so take all of the opportunities that life offers to build bridges to reach people. You can do this with a smile, an easy approach, and a positive, non-judgmental attitude.

Once you move closer to them, find ways to challenge people to overcome their self-doubt and use their special gifts to their best advantage in this world. Encourage everyone in your circle to create using their gift, whether they create new businesses, new books or works of art, or new ways to do things or new ways to heal and reach people.

Share ideas and listen to the ideas of others. Encourage brainstorming within the circles of people you are connected to. Teach and participate and grow together.

Look for solutions to issues that need solving, look for ways to make the world within your reach a little better and a little brighter every day.

And as you grow, be conscious that while self-empowerment will move you in directions you could never imagine, your ability to empower others will magnify your motion and reach.

When you blend empowerment with kindness, you will succeed beyond your dreams and take others with you to the new plains of achievement that will significantly change our world for the better.

Step Fourteen to Empowerment

The final step of the process is to understand that you are now empowered and to be able to use that strength and ability you have earned to propel yourself to your utmost development and empower others along the way.

If you ever doubt your strength again, be conscious that empowerment is not something you were given. It is something you earned and you must take because empowerment is the birthright of all human beings.

If you started reading this book and you were unhappy or dissatisfied with the dimensions of your life, you know now that you have the power to change your world.

All through this book I have stressed that there is only one purpose in life, and that is to find the means to empower others. You can only accomplish that when you find the means to live your life authentically, expressing yourself with your special gift and enthusiasm, doing work that appeals to you on every level.

True empowerment means finding the way to live your life so that you are filled with such a sense of purpose every day that what you do doesn't feel like work; it feels like life.

As a last step, imagine how you can get from where you are now to that special place where your unique gift can be used to enhance your life and the lives of those around you.

Now look at next week's agenda. What part of your schedule makes room for you to move closer to true empowered living? Move things around until there is a pocket of time every day, no matter how small it is, to propel yourself closer to living life empowered.

For every five minutes you can find to advance this life, it will be magnified by 100. That is the way empowerment grows.

If you do that, I promise you that by the end of this year, your life and how you live it will feel markedly different and more fulfilling.

ADDENDUM I

If you prefer to do your empowerment exercises all together, we have assembled each chapter's exercises here for you.

Step One to Empowerment:

Please take the time to answer these questions so that you will have a base to return to as you grow your empowerment. One of the essentials of moving forward is having a firm foundation and understanding your current sense of empowerment, however weak or strong it is, is important.

Question 1: How much do you feel in control of your life? You can gauge that by your responses to difficulties. Do they overwhelm you, or do you take them calmly in your stride?

Question 2: Do you recall a specific time in your life when you felt that fate was slapping you down, with each punch worse than the one before? Describe it briefly.

Question 3. What was happening to you and what part of your life was most impacted (family, business, relationships)?

Question 4. Have you experienced a time when you felt there was no way out?

Question 5. Do you believe that you can learn the skillsets to cope with life's ups and down better? Why or why not?

Step Two to Empowerment:

Question 1: Where is the path you are currently on taking you? Is that where you want to go? If not, are there options that you could embrace that would move you closer in the direction of the life you want?

Question 2: Have you recently had an experience where you were knocked down to the point that you felt powerless and numb? How did you find the courage to face another day? What thought reassured you?

Question 3: When was the last time that you learned something new? What was it and how has it helped you move further along your path?

Step Three to Empowerment: Your Learning Assessment

In your journal, write down all the formal and informal learning you have accumulated that helps you do your work and live your life.

Do you have learning that you are not using at this point? Is there a way to make it relevant in your life?

When you are looking at where you want to move in the future, what other learning do you need to be more effective once you get there? Is there a way you can start learning that even if you can't see a place to use it right now?

Step Four to Empowerment:

True empowerment is not a lightning bolt that hits you out of the blue and turns on your power. Rather, it is a gradual process of awareness that arises within yourself. It is a thread here and there that you pull, and some lead back to the fabric of your life, and others break.

In today's exercise, consider aspects of empowerment that can be learned from some of your own life experiences.

For example, what did you learn on your first job that changed your mind about how much power you had?

When did you first get a glimmer that there was a well of power within you if you could only figure out how to draw it out.

Write down some examples of moments that enlightened you about the idea of your own empowerment.

Step Five to Empowerment:

Change is tough, but it is living fully and authentically. Falling into the rut of routine without considering if it is still purposeful for you, as pleasant as it may appear on the surface, will rob you of your life a day at a time.

So many of us say that life is a journey, but we live it like we want it to be a destination. If you go through life doing one thing forever, never moving or changing or growing, you might as well say that life is static.

If you change your mindset to decide that change if your friend, that it is the trip to another place that you are looking forward to with excitement, you whole life starts to change.

You have a sense of empowerment that few can enjoy. Change is no longer tough; it is just another few miles ahead on the road of life. You don't have to figure it all out at once. You just have to think one thought, explore one aspect that doesn't please you anymore. How could you make it better?

In your journal today, trace the eras of your life in personal terms of careers posts, study terms, relationships, etc.

Now look at where you are today. What parts still ignite you? What parts still make you feel that there is a purpose to what you do? What parts don't excite you as you used to? What could you do (instead of complaining) to make them better? Do you have the resources to make the changes you'd like to make in your life?

How could you get those resources? Is there anyone who could help you? For example, if you want to go back to study, are their scholarships available or someone supportive at home to pick up a bit of the slack in day-to-day living?

What would happen if you dipped your toe in the water of change? Are you willing to risk it just to see where it could go?

What would that change be?

Step Six to Empowerment:

You are almost halfway through the process of securing your own empowerment, so it is time to become serious about what components would be needed for your life to be purposeful.

What kind of work makes you genuinely happy? If you had all the free time in the world, what would you do to fill your days? Is there a component of some kind of work in there? How would that work translate to a business offering?

Think about this in great detail. Look at what you love, and look at how it could be turned into a profitable business or career.

Do you need more training before you could go into it full time? How would you acquire that training? Would you be able to continue your current employment as you trained?

What does the market look like for the services or goods you would be offering if you were to open a business? What kind of similar businesses already exist? What could you do that is different or distinctive from them?

Do your research and keep notes about what you discover.

Step Seven to Empowerment:

It is time now to make a new life plan. Set your goals for moving towards the purposeful work you want to do and imagine how it will manifest itself. Will it involve establishing a business or securing a different job?

How long from this moment do you think it will be before you can turn your dream into a reality?

Will your family or loved ones support it? Why or why not? Can you find a way to work around your unique situation?

If it will involve a business, start now to create a business plan for your new venture.

The Business Development Bank of Canada offers business plan templates to help you if you need assistance. You can access them at:
https://www.bdc.ca/en/articles-tools/entrepreneur-toolkit/templates-business-guides/pages/business-plan-template.aspx

The CBDC offers a fillable PDF business plan option:
http://www.cbdc.ca/en/business-plan

74

You are now a "futurepreneur" and well on your road to empowerment!

Step Eight to Empowerment:

Who are the guides in your life and what have your learned from them?

Which ones do you consult regularly and how do they help you?

Do you believe their guidance is moving you in the right direction?

Who else could be your guide? How will you learn from them?

Are any of your guides unorthodox, like animals or trees or even those who report to you?

Step Nine to Empowerment:

Who or what do you place your ultimate belief in, other than yourself? Who do believe has your back?

Where do you go to fill up your well of power and energy? Is this resource plentiful and accessibly?

Write about your reservoir of strength until you are very clear about how it works in your life.

Step Ten to Empowerment:

This is the day that you need to ask yourself the hard questions about what you intend to use your personal power to accomplish.

There is no right or wrong answer to this question. It is against the natural law that we should judge each other, and not one of us has the right to judge the other.

So if you write down that you want to be empowered to fill up your bank account, that is what works for you and that is the kind of gratification you need.
If you write down that you want to be empowered just to fill up yourself so that you can live life fully and authentically, likewise that is a worthy goal.

If you strive for the highest form of empowerment, which is to empower yourself to empower others, then your life will be rich with purpose and energy and at the end of it all, you can lie on youth deathbed and say calmly to yourself, "I did good."

Take the time to establish your intent in this lesson. You are becoming more empowered with each lesson and each strategy that you choose. What will you do with your new knowledge?

Step Eleven to Empowerment:

Today it is essential that you define the tools that you will use to support your empowerment.

These are the values that you take to be true to yourself and that you will apply in deciding where to direct the power or force of your life.

I talked in this chapter about my values that I use as tools. Each person has different values, although some can be the same.

Pick four values that you place the highest value on as tools to support your empowerment.

Consider how you will summon them when you need to make life decisions. Are they of equal importance? Is one a priority and the others all of equal importance? It is important to think clearly about this, because these values and your empowerment will define your intent in life.

Step Twelve to Empowerment:

Practice the art of reframing life's challenges.

Look at the unwelcome change that has come into your life within recent weeks. Take it out as a separate component of your life and reframe it to show a different perspective.

How can this change be more positive? How can you reframe it to see it from an entirely different perspective?

Step Thirteen to Empowerment:

From this day forward, set aside at least two minutes a day to engage in an exercise of mindfulness.

Find a quiet place free from distractions. Slow your breath by inhaling and exhaling three times. If you have a natural essence that awakens your senses, inhale it at the same time.

Now observe life around you with clarity and without judgment. Try to stay focused just on the world around you.

If other thoughts creep into your reverie, gently guide them out and return to the present. If you start to judge your actions or the actions of others, help them exit as well and return calmly to your connection to the present moment.

You will find the daily practice of mindfulness to be the balance in your growth and continuing empowerment through life.

Step Fourteen to Empowerment:

The final step of the process is to understand that you are now empowered and to be able to use that strength and ability you have earned to propel yourself to your utmost development and empower others along the way.

If you ever doubt your strength again, be conscious that empowerment is not something you were given. It is something you earned and you must take because empowerment is the birthright of all human beings.

If you started reading this book and you were unhappy or dissatisfied with the dimensions of your life, you know now that you have the power to change your world.

All through this book I have stressed that there is only one purpose in life, and that is to find the means to empower others. You can only accomplish that when you find the means to live your life authentically, expressing yourself with your special gift and enthusiasm, doing work that appeals to you on every level.

True empowerment means finding the way to live your life so that you are filled with such a sense of purpose every day that what you do doesn't feel like work; it feels like life.

As a last step, imagine how you can get from where you are now to that special place where your unique gift can be used to enhance your life and the lives of those around you.

Now look at next week's agenda. What part of your schedule makes room for you to move closer to true empowered living? Move things around until there is a pocket of time every day, no matter how small it is, to propel yourself closer to living life empowered.

For every five minutes you can find to advance this life, it will be magnified by 100. That is the way empowerment grows. If you do that, I promise you that by the end of this year, your life and how you live it will feel markedly different and more fulfilling.

ABOUT THE AUTHOR

Kari Fulmek is the founder and owner of Equine Connection- The Academy of Equine Assisted Learning Inc., the world's only equine assisted facilitator training program that prepares participants to use their skills to operate their own business.

A Certified Master EAL Instructor and Certified EAL Senior Facilitator, she travels from her base in Calgary, Alberta to empower clients all over the world.

Kari started her company in 2009 as a single mother with three young children. With just a thought of what her ultimate dream in her life would look like. In its start-up stage, she watched in horror in one eight-week period when she had to cope with the death of four of her beloved horses and her mother, who was also her business partner.

She found the courage to rebuild and expand and today her reputation for excellence in her field and demand for her unique business offering stretches from Australia and New Zealand to Denmark, and from Europe and Scandinavia to the United States and Canada.

Along the way, she learned more than most of us will ever know about empowerment, specifically how to gain it and how to live a full life with it.

In this book, which follows Its Not Your DREAM If It's Not Hard, an earlier publication detailing her personal journey, Kari takes what she has learned about taking charge of her days and her destiny, and offers incredible insight we can all use to change our own lives with an attitude of empowerment.

Learn more about Equine Connection

Kari Fulmek's approach to empowerment can change your life. If you enjoyed her book and want to learn more about specific programs offered at Equine Connection, check out these sites.

My story: It's Not Your Dream If It's Not Hard
https://www.equineconnection.ca/freegiveaway
Our Website: https://www.equineconnection.ca
Our Team: https://www.equineconnection.ca/our-team
Our Certified Equine Assisted Learning Course:
https://www.equineconnection.ca/certified-equine-assisted-learning-course.html
Women's Workshop: https://www.equineconnection.ca/women
Team Building: https://www.equineconnection.ca/teambuilding.html
Curriculum Programs:
https://www.equineconnection.ca/youth-programs.html
Horses are Teachers: https://www.horsesareteachers.com

15742401R00049

Made in the USA
Middletown, DE
21 November 2018